TRIBUTES TO OUR ANGELS

FROM THE HEART OF A PARENT

SHANNON SPRUILL   TRACY PADILLA
TONJA NEWKIRK   TAMIKA MACLIN   MARILYN FOOTE
AKEA HOLLINGSWOTH

SMS WRITE ON PUBLISHING, LLC

ISBN: 978-1-7355437-5-8

CONTENTS

This is for every parent that has to live through losing child.

BRIAN MATTHEW

SHANNON SPRUILL

This is a story I have told before, but guess what, I am telling it again.

Brian Matthew Spruill was stubborn before he entered this world. I was almost one and a half weeks overdue. He was in no hurry to get here or, as I later discovered when he grew up; he had to make his grand entrance. Brian was always outspoken and driven. He had a vision and a plan, but God's plan was the one that was most important.

As a young child, Brian excelled in school. He was an outstanding student, with one exception; he talked too much. That reminded me so much of myself. My mother got the same report from my teachers. I believe he was not being challenged. The one thing he did enjoy was torturing his little brother. Brian was the middle child, but at times, he wanted to be the youngest. Other times, he acted like the oldest. They argued, but at the end of the day, they loved and protected each other. As I am writing this, the one thing I can clearly see right now is his infectious smile. He had a smile that would melt your heart.

When Brian was three years old, he broke his femur bone on his right leg. He was running and went to leap into the bed. As he was about to leap into the bed, he hit his leg on the metal bedpost. It was his upper thigh. The bone was protruding out. My husband held the bone done until the EMTs arrived. The EMT told him that holding the bone down actually saved his life. That was one of the longest nights of my life. I was 8 months pregnant with my youngest son and we were in the emergency room all night long. That was the first time I felt helpless as a parent/mother. They put him in trac-tion, but sitting there listening to my baby cry because of the pain was almost too much to bear. These are the tough moments that you can't prepare for as a parent. Your maternal instinct just kicks in and you find the best way to love and care for your children. I did not want to leave his side while he was in the hospital. My husband and I took turns staying overnight at the hospital. He was put in a full body cast and it was like going backwards for him. He had to go back to wearing diapers and once he came out of the body cast; he had to learn how to walk all over again. He bounced back like a champ. At a young age, he was resilient. Once Brian healed and was walking again, there were no lingering effects. Although Brian would often joke that he was lopsided now because one leg was shorter than the other.

As Brian grew older, he discovered he had a passion for fashion design. He went to college briefly but realized it wasn't for him. I was okay with that as long as he pursued something productive, like work. I knew Brian would be successful because he was driven and had determination. Not to mention he was extremely stubborn and selfish. I did not take a blind eye to my children's faults. When I was critiquing them, I was honest. This was the only way to get them to truly recognize their shortcomings. Brian told me he wanted to become a fashion designer. In the back of my mind, I thought, why not a lawyer, doctor or some other profession, but as a mother, I encouraged him to pursue his dreams. That is exactly what he did. He wrote a few articles for some fashion magazines and did several photo-shoots in New York, San Diego, Toronto and Chicago. He was beginning to live his dream; this is what I admired most about Brian.

Then one day, I could not see, hear, or touch my Brian any longer. He was gone.

How do you recover? From where do you draw

strength? These are a few of the questions parents ask after the loss of a child. Before October 4, 2013, I could only imagine how a parent might feel. Even trying to imagine was difficult. As a mother, you carry a child for nine months and you never think of losing that child. Journey with me as I discover how to live in spite of this devastating tragedy.

Thursday night, October 3, 2013, was an ordinary work night. I went to bed around 11:30 pm and slept soundly until 5:30 am, when my husband's phone rang. He did not answer it and then my phone rang. When I looked at my phone, I realized I had three missed calls from this same phone number. There was an unknown panic rising in the pit of my stomach. I answered the phone and the woman's voice on the other end asked, "Are you the mother of Brian Spruill?" I said yes, and she said, "You need to come to South Buffalo Mercy Hospital right away". I then asked, "What's wrong?" She responded, "You need to get here right away". At that moment, that sinking feeling in the pit of my stomach became real. My husband and I got dressed in silence and drove to the hospital in total silence. Anyone who knows us knows we are never silent when we are together. We dared not speak about what was lying on our hearts. I believe we were thinking about what was ahead of us. I think so many scenarios ran through my head. I just did not want to think about what I knew in my heart.

We arrived at the hospital and went to the security desk for directions to the emergency room. I don't know if it was just me, but the hospital lobby had an eerie and gloomy presence. The security guard walked us back to the emergency room. The woman behind the desk told the security guard she needed to walk us back to receiving room A. Walking down that corridor was the longest walk of my life, and it seemed like the hallway would never end. As she was taking us into the room, my husband asked, "what about our son?" She stated she needed to get the doctor to talk with us. As we entered the room, the first thing I notice was a pamphlet on the table with a candle on it and the pamphlet was for grief counseling. I knew, but refused to admit it.

The doctor came in with a nurse and sat down. She was a young, pregnant doctor. How ironic that she was about to bring life into this world. She said, "Your son, Brian, was in a serious car accident, and he was not wearing a seat belt. He was a passenger, and it seems the driver might have been speeding and they crashed into a cement utility pole." My husband said, "Well what about our son?" And she said, "I am sorry, but he did not make it." "I am sorry, but he did not make it", "I am sorry, but he did not make it". I just kept hearing that repeatedly in my head, trying to process what I was hearing. My world stood still, and my life completely changed at that moment. Today I still can't explain the range of emotions I felt at that moment. In my mind, I thought about God not giving you more than you could bear. I had changed my life, and I was serving God. I was not perfect, but I definitely made changes for the better. Through the initial pain, I wanted to trust God, but I was struggling. How do I make it back from this? Do I make it back from this? Where do I go from here?

My husband and I were left in the room to process this before going to see Brian. I was not able to process anything at that moment because I just kept hearing that doctor say he did not make it. It was like a record that kept skipping and repeating. I thought this was the beginning of me losing my mind. I have overcome so much, but I was not sure that I could come back from this. I lost my mother in 2010 and that was difficult, but the pain I felt from that loss did not compare. It was not the same.

As we went to see Brian, I hoped that he was not dead, and I would walk into that room and see my son smiling at me. As I walked through that door, I felt a rush of anxiety overtake me. He looked like he was sleeping. I wanted to say, "Brian, wake up now!!" My Brian was not waking up. I walked over and touched his hand; so cold. I touched his face; so cold. My baby was not waking up. He looked peaceful. He had a neck brace on, and the only visual sign of injuries was a small gash on his forehead. We stayed at the hospital for more than 5 hours. Family and friends came together and prayed. I met so many of his friends; they just kept coming. Seeing him lying on the hospital gurney was unreal. I could not process this in my mind. I felt the pain, but it just did not feel real. I just wanted Brian to get up and say something. It was almost noon and time for us to leave the hospital because they needed to transport him to the county medical examiner. The drive home was surreal. I still kept replaying that moment when the doctor said, "he did not make it". I don't think I will ever be able to get that out of my head. The irony was a pregnant doctor was about to bring life into the world while delivering the news of a life that has left this world. I still could not process the events that took place. I struggled to understand why this was happening to me.

I trust and believe in God, but at that moment, I was angry. The anger was building, and I started questioning God and wondering why God would allow this to happen. Was this my reward for committing to God? I was in the habit of praying daily, but this day, I could not pray. Anger kept me from talking to God. When we gathered in the room with Brian to pray, my mind was wandering. My mind and thought process were blurred. I needed to be busy. I kicked into gear, calling the funeral home, cemetery, and a lawyer. Keeping myself busy kept me from feeling or thinking.

The house started filling up with people, and this became my distraction. October 4th 2013, after everyone went home, it was just Esau, and I left to absorb what took place. We cried and held each other. Oh, how I welcomed sleep that night. I wanted to sleep so badly because my hope was when I woke up, I would realize that I had a horrible dream.

Wow, I just had a nightmare. I just dreamed that Brian was dead. I can't even repeat what I dreamed about. I just wanted to pick up the phone and call Brian. I dial his number and he answered on the third ring. I was so glad to talk to my son. Brian, I need to see you today. It was imperative that I saw him as soon as possible because that nightmare had me shook. "Mom, I will stop by after work". I would see my son soon. I went downstairs to tell my husband about my dream and the stairs led me into this dark, dank, dingy base-ment. When I reached the bottom of the steps, the steps disappeared. I was trapped in this place. I screamed, and no one heard my screams. I needed to get out of here because Brian was coming over after work. I suddenly saw a ghost-like image of Brian. I was speech-less and Brian spoke, "Mom I must go". Brian, you can't go! Please do not leave me!! And he faded away, and it got pitch black. Out of the darkness, there were hands coming out and surrounding me. I quickly sat up in bed, breathing heavily. I began to cry as I realized that I was dreaming. I felt like my world had ended. After that, I found it hard to sleep through the night and I was always awake at 5:30 in the morning. It was as if I had a built-in alarm clock.

I had a doctor's appointment and decided maybe I should talk to my doctor about my feelings and what happened. I told him what happened to Brian, but that was all. He said he was concerned about me and he wanted me to see a psychiatrist who specializes in grief counseling. When I left his office, I had every intention to go and see this doctor. I called her and made an appointment. I was not ready to express my pain to anyone. Even though she was a grief counselor, would she truly understand the depths of my pain? I just wanted to be left alone so I could ignore what I was feeling. For the first time in four years, I thought about smoking a cigarette and for the first time in many years; I thought about having a drink. My logic was so off because I felt like no matter how you try to live life correctly, you can't avoid the heartache that life brings. But I knew better because I was just looking for a reason to drink and smoke. It was just a thought because, deep in my heart, I wanted to do what was pleasing in the sight of God. It always came back to

God. Through the heartache, it always came back to God. Through the hurt and pain, it was God who I still wanted to please. Not fully trusting him right at that moment, I still had a need to please Him.

I needed to know why God would allow this to happen. I needed to search His Word and find some type of understanding and meaning to this tragedy. And most of all, why me?

Psalm 34: T*he Lord is nigh unto them that are of a broken heart; and saveth such as be of a contrite spirit.* There were so many scriptures about God providing comfort, but nothing about why God would allow you to go through such pain. In my heart I knew, but the pain prevented me from realizing what I already knew. I continued to search the scriptures for answers. Until this one scripture resonated within me, and I began to see things differently. Isaiah 43:2 *When thou passest through the waters, I will be with thee; and through the rivers, they shall not overflow thee; when thou walkest through the fire, thou shalt not be burned; neither shall the flame kindle upon thee.* God never promised that we would not endure trials, but he promised that he would be there with us to be a comforter. Then I thought of another bible verse I knew so well. John 3:16 *For God so loved the world, that he gave his only begotten Son, that whosoever believeth in him should not perish, but have ever-lasting life.* God himself knew what it meant to lose a child as He witnessed the crucifixion of His Son Jesus on the cross. These revelations did not erase the pain, but I was able to let go of some of my anger.

When I woke the following morning, all I could do was cry, but I could finally pray. I asked God to send his Holy Spirit to comfort me because I did not have the strength to deal with this. I needed to lean fully on God. I knew that my faith in God was the only thing to see me through this tragedy. I redirected my anger toward the young lady driving the car that night and the other passengers. They all survived. There were four people in the car that morning and only one that died was my son. I needed someone to blame, and a new anger arose within me. I was not angry with God any longer, but I was angry with the young lady driving the car. I just wanted my son to have a chance at life and I felt she took that chance away. Was she speeding? Was she drunk? What were the circumstances of the accident? I was instructed by my lawyer not to contact the young lady because it was now a legal matter, and they would contact her from now on.

I was so angry because none of the passengers in the car reached out to my husband or me. All I could think about is if that was me, I would want the parents to know that I was sorry. Not a word from the driver or other passengers. What were they thinking? Were they sorry? Did they even care? Once again, I took these feelings to God in prayer. I did not want the anger to fester. I needed to keep God front and center in my life at this time if I were to have any chance of surviving this ordeal. There was speculation that she was speeding, and it was raining that night. These details helped fuel the anger. But there was the Holy Spirit speaking to me, telling me to forgive. I was not ready to forgive, and I needed that anger at that moment. The anger also helped me to cope and deal with Brian's death. As long as I was angry, I had no room for any other emotions.

I started searching Brian's Facebook pictures to see if I could find this young lady. I found one picture of her with Brian and another friend. It felt like I stared at that picture for an eternity. I thought if I saw her face, I would find answers. At that point, I prayed. I needed to forgive this young lady because this was Brian's friend, and she did not get behind the wheel intending to kill Brian. But I was not ready to forgive because there was some sort of comfort in that anger and being able to have someone to blame. I put aside my feelings for a moment and imagined what she must be feeling. At that moment, I wanted to forgive her, but I still struggled. To this day, I have not met or seen the young lady, but my prayer is that she will find peace. I hope to meet her and let her know I don't blame her. I want that opportunity because she is the one who spent the last moments with Brian. I am hoping she can share those moments with me.

I understand how it feels when you think you are losing your mind. I understand how it would be easy to contemplate suicide. It's easy to sink into a never-ending depression. It is so easy to get lost during a time like this. I suffer from depression, and I was aware of where this could take me. I was trying to get myself ready for the biggest fight of my life and I accomplished this by realizing it was not my fight. I did not want to sink into depression because I know how hard that can be and this time; I was not sure if I could find my way back. I started having those feelings of impending doom and anxiety. I strapped in for this roller coaster ride of emotions.

I started researching grief following the loss of a child. I came across one article about a couple in the UK. Their nine-year-old son was killed in a crash. Their response to his death was heartbreaking. Below is an excerpt of the article by Auslan Cramb, Scottish Correspondent:

They remained by his hospital bedside for six days before they had to make the decision to turn off his life support machine. Weeks later his father Allan, 30, took his own life.

Kelly Hogg, 31, from Glasgow, who also has a 13-year-old daughter, said their son's death was more than they could bear.

She added: "Allan took his own life and died happy and content knowing that he was going to see his son again and that he would be there to look after him.

"It also gave me some comfort that my wee boy was with his daddy, who loved him more than anything in the world, and he wasn't out there all alone.

"I know it might sound strange to some people but when you are about to lose a child you love more than anything in the world, you want to do everything in your power to protect them. If that means taking you own life, then that is the sacrifice we decided to make."

Before Brian died, I might have called these parents crazy, but I learned that grief can affect everyone differently. The loss of a child can cause people to lose what sanity they have. But by the grace of God, that could have been me. That was not the answer, but I was so familiar with the pain. I found another interesting article by Carrie Gann, ABC News Medical Unit:

When her 19-year-old daughter, Amanda, died in a car accident in 1993, Susan Gilbert said her grief was exhausting. "I didn't sleep for a year. I slept for maybe half an hour a night," she said. "The experience is really beyond words."

Today, Gilbert works with other parents whose children have died, and said the loss affects all aspects of their lives. "While you do learn to live with it, you don't get over it," she said.

New research suggests that such parents can suffer devas-

tating, long-lasting health consequences as a result of the child's death.

The articles made me pause and think. As tragic as these stories were, something was missing. I do not know if any of these parents had a relationship with God, but I did know that there was a difference in these two stories. The first story of the couple seemed like hope was missing. The second story provided some hope. Susan Gilbert was so right when she said, "While you do learn to live with it, you don't get over it". I don't think I will ever get over the death of my son, but I am learning how to continue living and keep his memory alive. In my heart I knew it would be nobody but God who would see me through.

My pastor, (Pastor James R. Banks) shared something with me that week that I try to hold on to. He said, "You never stop feeling the pain, you just have to learn to live with it, it is okay to be angry, just don't stay there".

Good Grief:

Death is final, but grief is an ongoing evolution. It is necessary to go through the grief process to cope and live a fulfilling life. Progression promotes learning how to deal with your grief. There are many options to consider, such as group counseling, support groups, your church, books, etc. I think everyone has a different need, and it is important to find the right plan.

We know that no one lives forever, but when a loved one passes, we are still heartbroken. Nothing can truly prepare you to say goodbye. We miss their presence, impact, companionship, and love. Early in the grief process, it might be difficult to think about a plan. I believe during this time you should live out your emotions; be angry, question God, blame someone, question yourself, etc. Get this out of your system because it will become a hindrance in your grief journey. Do not avoid your feelings and emotions because they will eventually overwhelm you. Be prepared to hear all the cliché sayings; I know how you must feel, you will get over it in time, well at least you have other children, etc. Believe me, after hearing these so often you become angry, and you just wish that people would say nothing at all.

When grieving the loss of child, there can be long-term effects on the emotional stability of the parent. Along with hopeless comes the question, "what is my purpose in life?"

Part of my recovery was rediscovering who I was and discovering God's purpose for my life. I say rediscover because the day Brian died, my life changed forever. There are several steps in the grief journey.

1. Awareness. Recognize and admit your loss. Denial is very common during your grief journey. It is important to accept the reality of your loss. This will help you

up to get in touch with your feelings and emotions. During grieving, you may feel emotionless and unfocused. That is perfectly normal.

2. Work through your feelings and emotions. Do not bury what you feel; cry, scream and do what you need to do.

3. The next step is adjusting to your loss. Find ways to continue living and integrating the loss into your life. Redefine your life if necessary and, most of all, take care of yourself. So many times, grief can morph into physical and mental ailments. Make sure you are eating and getting enough rest. If you notice any physical or mental changes, make sure you seek medical attention. It is important to take care of yourself to be able to move through your grief journey. Of course, this is all easier said than done.

My health and eating habits suffered during my grief journey. I continue to struggle with health-related issues, but I am showing progress. I realized these habits were indirectly related to my grief. I think we all mentally prepare ourselves for losing our parents, possibly loss of a sibling, a friend, or a relative, but how do we wrap our minds around the thought of losing a child. The death of a child creates a pain that is unique to the individual parent. It is like you have been blindsided. Initially, there is numbness and shock. Especially if your child met with a violent death, you find your sorrow and anger too great for you to bear. You feel devastatingly guilty of not having been able to protect your child. You feel helpless. The complexity and confusion of your feelings may even convince you that you are "going crazy." I know after hearing all of this, you wonder how am I supposed to have hope? It is difficult, but it is possible.

If someone told me, I would be married with three children, I would have said no way. I had always dreamed of being a single businesswoman traveling the world. I never had a desire to have children. It was not in my game plan. I learned that God's plans trump all plans. I had to readjust my whole game plan and goals. It has been a journey seeking my purpose. I must surrender all to Christ to know my purpose. I am learning to appreciate my struggles as much as my success. I am grateful and better for the bumps along this journey called life.

I think of Brian every day. There is no dark cloud that consumes my life. I am not perfect or where I want to be, but there has been significant progress. I still can't sleep the whole night through. I still have moments where it is hard to focus. But I can say that I have hope and I have a God who is with me every step of the way.

Who is the new me? I am the woman who refuses to let depression find a home in me. I am the woman who will use her pain to help others. I am the woman who prays daily. I don't know what other valleys I will have to endure, but I know I will not face them alone.

Dutch Evangelist, Corrie Ten Boom quotes, "The measure of a life, after all, is not its duration, but its donation." I am looking to donate and make an impact. That is part of my new mission. I will share my experience and inspire hope in others.

Many think the mention of Brian's name will bring tears and sadness, but I am here to tell you that the mention of his name brings so much joy to my heart. I am a mother who lost a child, not a woman who lost her life because she lost a child.

2

NICI'S STORY

TRACY PADILLA

I never knew my heart could love so much. I never knew my heart could hurt so much. Nicolas Mathew Edenholm-Padilla, my only son, was born on Saturday, December 18, 1993, around 3:30 in the afternoon. The pregnancy was unexpected, and the labor was difficult. I was at a loss when they told me I was having a boy; I did not know how to raise a boy. But a boy I had, and boy did I love him.

As a newborn, he looked like a wrinkly old man. He was so sweet. I lived in Batavia, New York, with my daughter and my parents at the time. My daughter was 3 ½. My kids have been my whole world from the moment they were born. My calling in life was to be a mother, to take care of these little people who needed me so. Living with my parents with 2 kids was difficult. My Dad was older and had no patience for small kids or crying babies. I was so stressed trying to quiet my fussy Nicolas that he could feel the tension and fussed some more. I realized that my living situation was not working.

Richard is the father of both of my children. We were married when Nici was 13 months old. After the marriage, we all moved to Buffalo and the change in Nicolas was immediate. He was happier and seemed more at ease. Nici would take naps on my chest. As he grew older, I had to lay with him in his toddler bed, nose to nose, for him to fall asleep- one of my favorite memories.

Nici used to say he was going to marry me. Eventually, it changed to me being allowed to live next door to him and his wife. He made me laugh. He was a busy little boy who loved to terrorize his older sister, build with Legos, draw, and hunt for bugs. He loved all animals, from tiny insects to full grown beasts. He would go fishing with his father and spent most of the time setting the bait free. He didn't want to see anyone or anything harmed.

Every summer for 11 years, Nicolas, Brittany, and I would rent a cabin at a nearby campground. My sisters, nieces, and nephews would join. We would camp for a week or 2 at a time. Those camping trips, the family times, were amazing and unforgettable. I cherish those simple times beyond measure.

I have an older sister, Paula, who lives about an hour away. She has 4 children who grew up with my kids, as close as siblings. Nici and his cousin Ben were especially close. Whether it be at my house or Paula's, the kids would spend countless weekends and school breaks together. My kids were every bit a part of Paula's family, as hers were mine.

Some of my favorite memories included watching wrestling specials with Nic and up to 12 other little boys. Sometimes they would spend the night surprising Rich when he came home to see all the sleeping bodies on the living room floor. Sometimes I didn't even know their names. But I was always happy to entertain.

For as much as he loved nature, Mother Nature was not always was his friend. Nici was terrified of thunderstorms. At the first clap of thunder, he would be crawling into my bedroom, cautious not to wake my husband and be sent back to bed. I was always his safe spot.

I can recall another time when Nicolas tried his hand at farming. He was a young boy, about 8 years, and planted a small garden. When his "crops" were ready to be harvested, he attempted to sell his beans and tomatoes for $10 a piece. I ended up buying the entire crop for $30, a steal, but Nicolas was so excited to earn that money.

How much I love my son. I will always love him. There was nothing I wouldn't do for him or his sister. My Britt was brilliant and had good common sense. I didn't feel the need to be uptight watching over her; I knew she would be okay. I constantly worried about Nicolas making safe decisions. He was free-spirited and didn't always consider consequences of his actions. I worried.

Nicolas went to a charter high school, and it was an amazing fit. He wasn't so confident about heading into high school. He was quiet and reserved. After 4 years at the school, where they fostered creativity and different learning styles, he graduated a strong young man who was sure of himself, had a deep spirituality in nature, and matured on many levels. He met wonderful friends who found peace and comfort just spending time with Nic. His teachers, who praised his quiet contemplation and deep thinking, also adored him.

He was not a man of many words; he spoke little but said so much. Nici emanated peace and serenity. He was an old soul, inspired by music, especially Bob Marley. He appreciated harmony, nature, peace, and a good bowl of pasta.

Nicolas went to Italy for his senior trip. It was a life-changing trip, and he wanted to go back at some point.

He loved the cuisine, the culture, the creativity. That year, he also got a job at a Mexican restaurant. He met many friends there, but was closest to a young man named Zach. He also worked at a friend's father's plant making supplements. So, plant work by day, restaurant work at night, the boy was barely home. He was dedicated to his work. I would wait up for him to get home, having some sort of special meal ready, despite the late hours. We would sit and chat for a bit while he ate. How much I miss those simple times.

After a while, Nic left the restaurant to work full time at the plant. He spent most of his time with a good friend, Shane. The first time I met Shane, he called me Mom. I was hooked. He loved my food and was a common guest at my house. I once again was able to entertain like I did on those wrestling nights all those years ago.

Nicolas and his friends were often seen playing hacky sack and riding bikes around town. He didn't have his license, but had just begun studying for his permit. He never got the chance to take his driver's test.

The summer of 2014 was filled with mishaps for Nic. I found out a few of these after he passed. Like how he had been clipped by a car when riding his bike. Or had passed out while mowing the lawn with my husband, hitting his head on the mower. On July 4, I got a call at work. Nicolas has cut the tip of his finger off at work. I took him to the hospital for stitches. On our way home at 4AM, he thanked me for taking him and staying with him. He never had to thank me for such things. I told him how much I loved him. How this was my job to be by his side. A job that never felt like work.

This brings us to the first week of August 2014. I woke up on that Monday feeling very unsettled. So much so that I made an appointment with my doctor to discuss medication. Tuesday night, Nici came home and told me he had been invited to a camping trip in the Adirondacks with some friends. At the time, he was unsure if he wanted to go. Given my recent increased anxiety and feelings of something being wrong, I had asked him to please stay home. Rich and I spoke about it and neither of us wanted him to go, but he was 20 years old, so we couldn't just forbid it.

Wednesday he came home and said he wasn't going. I was so relieved. The following day, Brittany, who never calls into work for anything, took the day off for herself. We planned to visit my family that afternoon. I went into Nici's room to see if he would like to come with us, only to find him packing. I asked what he was doing, and he said, "Mom, I have a few days off of work and Zach keeps bugging me so I guess I'm gonna go." I asked him to come with me instead, but he seemed resigned to go. I knew he didn't want to. I wasn't happy, but I helped him pack and asked what time he was leaving. He answered sometime in the afternoon, and Zach was driving. I begged him to find a way to call me, given the terrible service out that way. When it was time for Britt and I to leave, I got a hug, a kiss, and an "I love you." I told him to please be careful. Then he turned to Britt, whom he always called "Sis" and gave her a hug, a kiss, and an "I love you," as well. That interaction was not so typical for my children. I later found out that Nici spent the rest of his morning visiting friends, almost like a goodbye. I think he felt something.

Throughout the day, I kept in touch with Nic. They finally got on the road about 5:30. I talked to him for a few minutes until his phone stopped working. Still feeling unsettled, I kept trying to call him back, but there was no response. I was inconsolable on Friday. I prayed and begged God, "Please bring Nicolas home," over and over. My mention of these fears at work on Friday night and Saturday morning, only to be met with mocking and told to "Cut the cord." I was scared, and I continued calling his phone. Saturday morning, I called my sister and told her I knew something was going to happen to Nick. I wanted her to pray with me. Her exact words to me were, "I hope he doesn't slip and fall and drown." To this day, she does not remember saying this, but I will never forget. I responded, "Oh my God, Paula! No!" Despite my unsettled feelings, this thought had not crossed my mind.

I continued working and continued calling Nic's phone. I even checked with some of his friends to see if they heard from him at all. All the answers were "no." At about 2:40 PM, I finally got to leave work. I was walking to my car and a strange number popped up on my phone. I don't typically answer unknown numbers, as they are usually scams, but this time I did. It was Nicolas!

He had found a pay phone. The minute I heard his voice, I cried. I breathed. It felt like I had been holding my breath up to that point. "Oh my God, Nic, I have been so worried about you!" I told him. His voice cracked as he responded, "I know, Mom." I asked if he was having fun and he said, "Oh yea!" He told me he was with some of Zach's friends, and he would be home Tuesday. I worried about him being hurt by an animal and asked him to please stay on a campground and not just somewhere in the wild. He promised he would. He said, "Love you," and promised to call again.

It elated me after I heard from him and I called everyone to let them know he was okay. I made a special pasta and watched Godzilla, thinking of Nic the entire time. When Nic was little, he and I watched all the Godzilla and dinosaur movies together.

About 10:30 that night, I saw the headlights of

someone pulling into the driveway. I was excited because I thought Nic had come home early! The thought of him being home early made me so happy. I ran to the door to greet him. I opened the door and instead of seeing my beautiful son; I saw police officers standing on my porch. They asked if I was Nicolas Padilla's mother. I said, "Yes." I started screaming, "Where is Nicolas?!" They asked if my husband was home. They suggested I get him. I also screamed for Brittany, who lived in our upstairs apartment with her boyfriend. She ran down the stairs and Rich ran into the living room. They asked if we knew where Nicolas had gone. After replying, "Yes," they told us Nicolas, my sweet baby boy, had drowned. Richard fell to his knees. I argued that it wasn't true, it couldn't be true. I had just spoken to him a few hours prior. All I could say was, "No. No. No. No." Britt just stood in shock. They said they had some information for us which Rich took down. They asked if we wanted them to stay, but of course we didn't. We all cried and hugged each other. Richard, Brittany, Joey, and I were all in shock. Brittany called my sister to tell her what happened, but couldn't get ahold of her. She tried Paula's daughter. As soon as she heard a, "Hello," she yelled into the phone, "Nici died! He drowned! Please have your mom call us!" Paula called us back shortly after, in just as much disbelief as us. She insisted, "No, everything is fine!" I snatched the phone and said, "Nicolas is dead." I called my mother, and she then called the rest of my siblings. Within an hour, my entire family was by my side.

I don't remember too many details from the rest of that night. Britt said I sat on the sidewalk and wailed and sobbed. It surprised her no one called the police from all the noise. Eventually, everyone left except for Paula and her husband, Scott. They offered to drive us to Long Lake to claim my son's body.

We all tried to get some sleep before our long drive. I laid in Nick's bed but could not sleep. I got up and talked to Paula. We shared one of Nic's specialty yogurts as we spoke. We got on the road around 5:30 AM that Sunday, with Scott driving, Paula in the front seat, and Britt, Rich, and myself snug in the back. It was an absolutely beautiful day. How dare the weather be so perfect when our lives had just been torn apart? In the back seat, we held hands and cried. Every time we stopped to get gas, we saw stands selling honey, one of Nic's favorite things. At his job, they had bee hives and Nic would sit there and eat honey right from the comb.

Hours later, we arrived at the hospital. An officer there filled us in on some details. Nic and Zach had climbed to the top of Buttermilk Falls and crossed at the top. The rains had been heavy, leading up to that day, making the current strong and the water high. Zach made it across. Nicolas did not. He tripped on his way over and hit his head on the rocks. We were later told that he must have instantly passed out. When he fell into the water, the current pushed him under the falls and under sticks, trapping him in place. This all happened over an hour after I spoke to him. Later, someone local told me they didn't even know of any payphones in the area. That was strange. Apparently, other swimmers and bystanders tried to help pull him out, but to no avail. The current was just too strong. It took them over 4 hours to recover his body. It took another 2 plus hours for us to be informed. We were told that Zach was in shock, having just witnessed his friend pass in front of his eyes and being unable to help.

It took them a while to bring us down to the morgue, but it was finally time to see him. Rich and I went in. Britt hesitated, took a step in, and collapsed. Paula and Scott were by her side and helped her leave the room. Rich and I stood over what was left of our son. He looked like he was sleeping. They covered one side of his head with a white towel. That must have been where he hit the rock. He also had a thin bruise encircling his neck. I was told that was probably how they pulled him out. We talked to Nic. We touched him and kissed him and brushed his hair with our fingers. But I knew in my heart that this shell no longer housed my Nicolas.

We talked to the coroner on our way home and

made arrangements to have Nicolas returned to Buffalo. Other phone calls were made and received. One was from the manager of the restaurant Nici worked at. He gathered the employees and met us with loads of food upon our arrival. Not that any of us were really hungry. Lots of people came to the house that day and on the days that followed. I met some of Nic's friends. Zach hadn't come yet. He stayed in the Adirondacks another day. But he came the next day with Nici's belongings. We cried and hugged. He expressed his condolences.

When arranging services, we decided on a cremation and purchased a beautiful, weeping angel urn. We held the wake and funeral simultaneously. It was a Thursday night and over 700 people attended. The line was out the door. We couldn't all fit in the room. Rich, Britt, and some other family and friends spoke about Nicolas.

A few days after the service, Nicolas came to me in a dream that didn't feel like a dream at all. He hugged me and told me he was so sorry and that he was okay; such a Nici thing to say.

We only saw Zach the one time at the house and again at the funeral. I begged him to talk to me, to fill me in on the mundane details of their trip. I wanted to know everything. But he stopped responding to me. I hated him. I blamed him. Even though I knew it wasn't his fault.

After all is said and done, I absolutely believe that it was Nic's time to go. There were too many coincidences. I think he sensed it, too.

I have some really dark times, but somehow, I have survived each day. I try to do good deeds in Nic's name. I think he would like that. My life now consists of cherishing my family. I have a 5-year-old grandson who looks just like my sweet son, Nicolas. I also have a sweet and mischievous 20-month-old granddaughter. I am a full time Grammy and watch the kids while my daughter works. They are what keeps me going.

Our family seems to have settled into a quiet life. We try to honor and remember our beautiful Nicolas as much as we can. His urn sits on my dresser and I talk to him every day. I kiss the wings of the angel, hoping he can feel it on his face. The pain of losing him will never go away, but I thank God every day that I was chosen to be his mother; that I got to spend 20 glorious years with him.

I love you dearly and miss you every second my Nicolas. HAK (Hugs And Kisses).

3

FROM TRADEGY TO TRIUMPH

TONJA NEWKIRK

*D*eQwaun LaMarc Newkirk was born on Saturday, April 9, 1988 at 2:46pm at Children's Hospital. DeQwaun was my only child and the half-brother to 5 other siblings. DeQwaun was known as Qwaun, Fatman, and Qwainie bear and a few other nicknames. DeQwaun attended Bennett High School, in Buffalo, NY, for his freshman year and later transferred to Kenmore West High School where he enjoyed playing football. It was during his high school years that DeQwaun pledged to the Junior Iota Phi Theta Fraternity, Incorporated (Jr IAO). While in high school, DeQwaun stayed busy with many community activities. DeQwaun was known for being the DJ at community dances.

DeQwaun thought about his future and started looking into what career he would follow. The path DeQwaun would soon pursue was with construction. DeQwaun became certified as an Occupational Safety and Health Administration (OSHA) representative. He became a Certified Asbestos Supervisor and a Certified Demolitionist through New York State. DeQwaun was working on building his own company called Gifted Hands because of his many talents with his hands.

DeQwaun loved to fellowship or party as the young folks like to call it. He enjoyed being with family and friends, where good food, good music and fun were a necessity. DeQwaun especially enjoyed spending time with his sons, DeQwaun Lamarc Newkirk Jr.(11 years old) and Zy'ir Johan Newkirk (4 years old). DeQwaun was engaged to Dainna Ford and son Naz'ir Austin (7 years old). His family meant the world to him, as he would always speak highly of them. DeQwaun faced some challenges in his short-lived life. He lived, loved and managed disappointments with grace and trusting the God of his understanding.

DeQwaun also spoke of how he saw hope for a better tomorrow in the eyes of his children. DeQwaun was a devoted father, son, fiancé, uncle, brother, nephew, and grandson. Sadly, on April 25, 2019, at 5:47am, gunshots would break my morning sleep and forever alter my world. Our home would never be the same because this is the last day I would see DeQwaun's warm, handsome face.

DeQwaun was my only son and to have him taken from us at such a time in his life when he was finding himself and making great positive progress in his life was a tragedy.

DeQwaun was raised in church and it was there that his talents would start to bloom. DeQwaun played the drums by ear. I would later place him in drum classes at the African Cultural Center. It was there that DeQwaun played for one of our past President of the United States of America. It was then I knew he was destined for greatness. DeQwaun was the love of my life and although he was not perfect, he was my son and I loved him unconditionally. My life has changed so much since that dreadful day.

I have reached back to what has always gotten me through, and that is to my God. Let me say that it was a process for me to get to where I am now. I would be restless all night and then get up and get dressed for work and on my way to work I would log on to Facebook and do what I call my morning motivation. But really it was me speaking to myself so that I wouldn't lose my mind. I would use my time doing that and what I learned is others needed to see my pain, see me go through and see that I have good days and bad days but I was still living and working after such a terrible crime.

One day while doing my Facebook live I spoke into my own life. I told the world that "you can be strong and weak at the same time." It was then I knew I had to tell my story. It has been two years now and I still find myself looking back at the videos I created and the words I spoke then still stand today.

DeQwaun was always one to love the limelight and I not so much. I enjoy being in the background. Today I find strength despite losing my only child and if I can make a difference in this world it would be by giving back. On May 29, 2021, we had our first Memorial Cookout in honor of DeQwaun my hero. I no longer grieve his life. I now celebrate all that he stood for. I am in the process of carrying on his business, Gifted Hands LLC (in my name in honor of DeQwaun) and it will be a not-for-profit that will distribute scholarships for our young men and women in the construction field.

Because of DeQwaun I am learning and embracing my gifts and looking forward to sharing them with the world. Attached to Gifted Hands LLC will be a counseling component, with a focus on trauma; repairing and healing our youth and young adults, especially African Americans. I am a Mental Health Counselor with my Master's degree in Clinical Mental Health Counseling and I am pursuing my license.

I will end my brief chapter with a Quote: "Death leaves a heartache no one can heal, love leaves a memory no one can steal." Richard Puz

4

LANASHA NICOLE ROLLERSON

TAMIKA MACLIN

*L*anasha Nicole Rollerson was a blessing sent straight from God. I remember carrying her at the tender age of 16. I didn't know how I would take care of her or how to be a mother. Still in High School, I was so embarrassed to be 16 and pregnant; I eventually dropped out of school months later after finding out I was pregnant. Not only did I drop out of school, I walked away from the church because I was ashamed, and I didn't want to be judged. However, I knew Lanasha was a blessing from God, a rare gem, and that she would be something great in life!

While carrying Lanasha, after I left the church with no intentions of returning, my best friend invited me to joy night at church. Joy night was a youth service, and I absolutely loved youth service. I agreed to go to the service this one time. Still, to this day, I'm grateful that I went to service that night. That night, we had a guest speaker who came all the way from North Carolina. I don't remember what she preached about, but I will always remember what she whispered in my ear. The guest speaker finished preaching, and she had an altar call! I remember getting up at the last minute, being the very last person in line. The guest speaker hugged me tight and whispered in my ear that God had something special for the child I was carrying. I believed her from the bottom of my soul because she didn't know me, and you could tell I was pregnant. As a teenager, I was 5'11 inches tall and very thin. From that day forth, I knew Lanasha was going to be a doctor, lawyer, or something special.

June 6th, 2000 I gave birth to my first-born child, Lanasha Nicole Rollerson. She was a beautiful baby with straight black hair. When they laid her on my chest, I fell in love with her. I only wanted the best for her.

I always kept Lanasha in some kind of church activity, even when I didn't attend church. Lanasha loved God! She had many questions about God and she loved to study about God. Lanasha also never gave up on me. She begged and prayed for me to go back to church. Her prayers were answered when she turned 10. She was so excited.

Lanasha loved to laugh and be silly! She often greeted me at the door with a scare when I would come home from work. I used to get so mad at her for that. But she got me every time. She loved to draw; she was very creative. Lanasha did a drawing at school when she was younger; she named it watermelon the chameleon. It was so unique that the school put it in the school calendar. She loved to do nails, too!

She was athletic! She ran track and played basketball. I remember being at her first track meet. We invited friends and family. We all sat together in one area and cheered her on. I'll never forget her taking the lead in her first meet. She made it 2 steps before the finish line. She could hear us cheering for her, and she stopped and started cheering with us. Then we all started yelling at her to finish the race. She was so close, but she was being silly and before we knew it, another student beat her just that quick. However, Lanasha learned a valuable lesson that day.

Lanasha loved to cook, bake, and eat. I remember the first day she cooked the family a meal. I was working when she was at home with my mom and her siblings. When I got home, dinner was made. She did an excellent job. Because she knew she did an excellent job, she continued to cook more. At this time, she was 11 years old. Lanasha also loved people. She would be friends with anyone. She understood people. Sometimes I thought she was too friendly. She even loved the people who treated her wrong and were not loving to her. She never gave up on anyone.

Lanasha also had struggles at a young age. Struggles that many young women experience and hold it in for years and sometimes even death. I share Lanasha's struggles with you, hoping to heal and setting yourself free from any struggles that you may have experienced or are experiencing. Lanasha was also keeping an enormous secret that was eating away at her every day. I would never understand what she was going through until it was too late.

April 13, 2013 Lanasha was very sick. So sick we went to the emergency room. It was then that she revealed to me that she was raped over a year ago. I'll never forget the cry from her gut. In my heart, I knew she was telling the truth. I remember telling her when the nurse came back in we were going to let her know and that whoever it was would go to jail. We would make a police report and have a rape kit done on her. They made me leave the room for a while and I called a close, trusted family member in to see what other steps we may need to take.

I couldn't understand how I missed the signs. I tried to protect her. I never let her go too far from where I could see, and I left her with trusted family members when I went to work. How could something like this could happen? That day we left the hospital, things were never the same. She asked for help because she was really suffering. I called to make appointments with mental health counselors and getting her an appointment was very hard. We finally made an appointment, but it was not until September.

Not long after that, things spiraled out of control. I remember getting a phone call from the school telling me they were going to expel her and 2 of her peers because she was smoking marijuana in the school bathroom. I never thought that her being raped would lead her down such a hard road because I compared her story to my story, and I didn't behave the same way. She would go to church on Sundays and every Sunday she would be at the altar pouring her heart & soul out. I allowed her to release that way because that was the only way for her to release her hurt and pain.

July 4th, 2013 I found her diary, and I was shocked! The things I found out that day I was so heartbroken. I couldn't believe my eyes. However, once again, because I thought she should heal a certain way, I wasn't understanding the struggles that she dealt with after being raped. Summer continued, and she wasn't able to do anything but play basketball in the backyard. I thought things would get better for her. However, Lanasha was 13, and she wanted to hang out with her friends. I was too scared to allow that because I didn't know what would happen to her. My fears were playing out right in front of my eyes. I needed Lanasha to understand that she would be ok and that her story was not that bad. So we read the book of Job. I wanted her to have an example of someone who lost everything and still could put faith in God and live.

In mid-August I was invited to watch a play. I wanted her to go with me, but it didn't turn out that way. I went with my 1-year-old at the time while she and her siblings went out. The play was about a young boy having family issues and he left the house. Suddenly I could feel Lanasha all over me. She wasn't there, but I felt her. The young man in the play went missing for 3 days before they called for a break. My son was getting tired and started to whine, so I decided I would leave so he wouldn't disturb the surrounding people. I walked to the back where all the vendors were and God stopped me in my tracks. I waited a little while longer and the play started over. Because I was in the back, I could see the play unfold right in front of my eyes. I looked to the left of me and I watched the people in the play bring out a lifeless body of the child they searched for, for 3 days. It hit me in my gut and I began crying because I could still feel Lanasha on me. I didn't understand, but I knew to pray. I left the play that night and I knew that me and Lanasha had to have a one-on-one conversation. The morning after the play, I got

Lanasha up bright and early so we could talk in private. As we made our way to the store that morning, I told Lanasha about the play I saw and how I felt her; I assured her that would not be her story. From the day I told Lanasha about the play, she had this unusual calmness about her. She didn't want to be bothered by many, and she seemed so at peace. Starting August 29th, Lanasha began to make connections with the people she was closest to, and it gave her so much joy.

Sunday, September 1, 2013, I woke up early. School was starting, and we had a celebration to be at that evening. I woke up and went upstairs to check on my 2 girls, but Lanasha wasn't there. I asked my other daughter where Lanasha was, and she said she didn't know. My heart sank, and I searched the house, but she was nowhere to be found. Because it was Sunday, I told myself she went to church with her Grandmother because it was not odd for the girls to wake up on a Sunday very early and go to church with their Aunt or Grandmother and not say anything because they left that early in the morning. I tried to calm myself, so I washed her clothes and wait for her and her grandmother to come from church. I could hear a commotion in the driveway, so I sent my daughter to meet Lanasha at the door. I could hear my daughter dart down the hallway, up the stairs and out the door. Moments later, I heard her open the door and come down the stairs, darting down the hall again. She said Mom Lanasha didn't go to church. I immediately went into panic mode. I called the police, and the search began. My family, friends, and the community helped search for her. We searched for 3 days for Lanasha with no police assistance. We asked questions, put up flyers and looked throughout the neighborhood.

The first night she was missing, it began to rain and my body just went weak. I knew something was wrong. Lanasha was missing the celebration, and it was raining. It wasn't like her to not come home. I stayed home while everyone else was looking and I remember falling into a deep sleep. I dreamed of her the first night. She stood in the dark of night with basketball shorts on and a white shirt and she said I just wanna come home. That woke me up out of my sleep. I called my sister as soon as I woke up. It was 6:02 am I asked her if she was still looking and she said she was headed home to take a nap and go back out. I told her to come get me when she woke up.

It was 8 am on Labor Day and we began the search again. We received a phone call that night that would change everything. The next morning was crazy. It was like we were being sent on a wild goose chase. Finally, the police got involved but one of the first things they did was call us and tell us to go home and wait for them to call us; they were taking over the search. They also told us if we go within the premises they would take us to jail. We went home and waited. It got dark, and I felt the same way I felt while watching the play. At that point, I lost all hope. I knew the outcome wouldn't be in my favor. My friends were visiting and comforting me. Then I told them I was going in. I went in the house and my family was coming from a youth revival that night and finally the news reported that my daughter was missing. As that played on the television, my sister-in-law said to me they prayed for Nay Nay tonight. She also said that another woman pulled her to the side and told her you're going to find her swiftly and be prepared.

It finally hit me. My daughter was never coming home. I had a side conversation with God in my head. You took her, you really took her, you said you had something special for her and she is gone… Bang, Bang, Bang was the knock at the door; it took me out of my trance. My niece began to yell, "Auntie, they found her, they found her." I dashed out the door and we went to the place they said she was. It was right around the corner. From a distance I can see the yellow tape and police cars. I told my sister don't take me up the street. I refused to see my daughter coming out in a body bag. It took hours for the coroner to get there. As I sat in the distance, I saw the coroner's van ride up the street and it eventually came back down the street and rode right by me. A detective then came down the street to talk to me to tell me I had to ID the body in the morning. But after questioning the detective, I knew it was my daughter. I was officially living my worst fear. I woke up that morning and we headed to the morgue. We had to wait awhile but once we finally got to view her, it was confirmed; my daughter was laid out on a cold steel bed, lifeless. I can never explain how I felt after that. The pain was unimaginable. I wouldn't wish it on my worst enemy. Someone stole my child's innocence and then her life. She is forever 13.

I suffered in silence for years after Lanasha was murdered. I felt I had to hold it together for my children and my family. I was a mess and was holding it in every day, letting the pain just bubble up. Eventually, I was diagnosed with anxiety. The anxiety attacks were horrible, my emotions were off, and I also had brain fog. I honestly don't know how I made it through. Until I started praying, I began to pray for healing and that is when God gave me meditation, which led to affirmations, then I finally went to therapy. After that, I was able to start my healing journey. I could find peace and calm in the midst of my storm. A renewing of the mind happened. I'm forever grateful for the journey I was able to take for my healing. I also want to add I still deal with the pain of the loss of my daughter, I just deal with it differently. I know different techniques that will not allow me to just sit in the pain and struggle with anxiety. It is my prayer that someone reads this and knows that there you still have life after dealing with traumatic and painful experiences that you have in life. Never give up on yourself, you are worthy of a fulfilling life. To end our story, I know why Lanasha was placed here on earth. As much as it hurts me to say, Lanasha served her purpose here in life. She was sent to me for a short period of time but the lady who told me God has something special for her didn't lie. I just didn't understand the mission until she was no longer with us. It hurts me each and every time I share our story. However, I know the mission is greater than us both. It's my purpose to share & remember the horrible things we have to face to help others experience healing after the storm.

5

MY LOSSES TURNED TO GAINS

MARILYN FOOTE

Excerpt from Book, 'The Foote-Paths in My Career'
©March 2021

2 Corinthians 4:16-18
New International Version
"16 Therefore we do not lose heart. Though outwardly
we are wasting away, yet inwardly we are being
renewed day by day. 17 For our light and momentary
troubles are achieving for us an eternal glory that far
outweighs them all. 18 So we fix our eyes not on what
is seen, but on what is unseen, since what is seen is
temporary, but what is unseen is eternal."

*G*od intertwined into my spirit these verses as I studied my Bible lessons, growing up. As a teen, young in my calling, I initially was unsure of the source of my quiet assurance. I would later understand these words' profound meanings; helping me focus on what is unseen rather than my situation. This resulted as a blessing, using my life to be a light to others.

Embracing their special essence, this is my story about the deaths of two of my foster children; a teen, and a young adult and the emotional pains of losing five emergent fetuses during my child-rearing years. But, my story does not just sit right there. It is a coping experiential recount because I believed and still am sure that God was deep within my life walking along with me through all the emotional roller coaster I was going through. Also, my story is not bragging about how I stood steadfast to His words and lived a pure, wholesome life. I accepted Jesus as my Lord and Savior at an early age, and my walk with Him while I matured and developed as I grew. I was making mistakes as I lived, but each day I would get on my knees to confess my sins and asked for forgiveness. Then, I would meditate on His words to help me prepare my heart to do better the next day. This was a repetitive process that never stopped guiding me to be more God centered and finding Godly peace. Amen.

MY FAMILY

This is the make-up of my complete family. My two children I birthed and still living are Lisa and Tatchy. My foster children I cared for when I lived in the country of the Ivory Coast, in West Africa (also known as Cote d'Ivoire) are Lydie, my step-daughter, my nieces and nephews, Isabelle, Guy Marie (Pélé), Odette, and distant relatives François, Mary, Chantelle, and Ahou. Also, my last foster child I cared for was an American great-nephew, Donald. Deceased are: François; he was a young adult and Isabelle when she was a teen. I miss-carried five pregnancies during my child rearing times: Summer, 1973; in May 1978 flying over the Atlantic; at school, International Community School of Abidjan (ICSA), 1980 summer; and Dec. 1981. I listed all my children because I wanted to show you how God filled my motherly passion with many others to love after the losses.

MY STORY

I was raised in a large family of eight children, a father, mother, grandfather. I cherished my siblings' interrelationships so much that when I was young, often I dreamed of having a large family of my own. This was one of my early prayers for my future, and to also have a husband. When that time approached, my fiancé and I agreed to try for a large family. Being so full of youthful dreams on what joys of producing those cute and cuddly bundles was going to happen that I could not imagine that life would set-up a series of discouraging situations to contest every effort I made.

My husband was from Ivory Coast, which resulted in an unforeseen cultural clash. Initially, he spoke like his six plus years of American exposure had influenced him, having observed different parenting styles. It was not enough to change his understanding of how a present father should be. He was mindful at times about being a fully involved parent and it showed once in a while on what he did with his children, but his deeply rooted career goals caused him to play a different tune when he returned to his country.

Like I, he desired a large family, but he believed that his main contributions to our effort was to biologically father the babies and to financially provide support and maintain his family. He would stay in the trimming and boundaries of a family, not necessarily involved in the daily inn keeping. The everyday up-keep belonged to the woman. In his culture's eyes, he was a present father and issues arose when we talked for long hours about this. Soon I realize that he had not made this clear to me.

I learned that the woman should lean on her female family members or girlfriends to encourage her and help for most of the essential parts of raising a family. I adapted and embraced my new customs. I also connected to a network of American ladies living in the main city of Abidjan, which became a unique tribal group that supported each other. We even took a humorous stance on some of our newly inherited traditions, placing healthy boundaries we swore by to include our special conditions. My husband raised his eyebrows at a few of the particular situations, like requiring his present at the children's school programs and teacher meetings like my dad and grandfather did. I insisted it was a strong traditional custom in my American family. My friends would stand in the background nodding their heads in agreement.

So, we moved past our differences and started working on our family. Sadly, the pattern of miscarriages started early. I lost one just before we married. I was experiencing conflicting thoughts about my situation. Was I to wait to start my family? What was I to do about the birth control risk factors? Or was I right in being sexually active? Since I felt that my effort to have a large family was mainly God's anointing, I prayed continuously asking for His blessings. We married. We were a little worried that the combination of events that started in 1973 with my first miscarriage was going to shape our future. I had just finished my college Bachelor's degree in Education and my husband needed one more year to complete his Master's in Business Management and Administration (MBA). So we thought that maybe we should wait for our schedules to settle down before trying again.

I struggled with birth control. During the two previous pregnancies, I was using a birth control called the Dalkon Shield, which was an IUD with an above average safety rating, but found it was not an effective combination for me. The reason was recorded for my first miscarriage in 1973 was this device and the doctor prescribed another form of the shield IUD called the "Copper T" IUD. This method was short-lived. Soon after, the doctor tested me to discover I was pregnant. He laughed, stating that my body was actually pushing the "T" out. I did not use any IUD again and my beautiful baby girl, Lisa, was born.

The IUD contributed to my miscarriages but was not the cause. The actual cause surfaced later, sadly after several more lost pregnancies. My doctor in Abidjan, Dr. Koné, discovered that in the first trimester (the first three months of the pregnancy), I had a major drop of estrogen hormones, which caused my body to struggle to support a baby. As a result, the fetuses died and came out. I carried one baby up to the fourth month, but my hormone counts dropped again and the embryo died.

The pairing of two doctors communicating across the Atlantic Ocean, one in the Abidjan, Ivory Coast, Dr. Koné and the other in Buffalo, New York, Dr. Chouchani were the lifesaving team that assisted me with my last full-term pregnancy. This had to happen because I was on a limited time constraint, staying only one month in Buffalo after my fifth miscarriage, and I had to return home to Ivory Coast. This special partnership nurtured me and I gave birth to my son, Tatchy.

Despite the difficulties of having babies plague me; my family grew, and grew, and grew with what I called God's blessings. My prayers were answered with God bringing other foster children for me to love. With my first born arriving in Ivory Coast, in 1976, my family increased three fold. They were relatives of my husband; François, a 15-year-old boy, my step-daughter Lydie, five-years-old, and Ahou, a ten-year-old girl.

I remembered when Lisa was two and a half; I over-heard my brother-in-law talking to my husband about his son who lived in the village. He was just a year older than Lisa. He could not afford to pay for the school fees and uniforms. They spoke the conversation in Dida, their tribal tongue, but for some reason I picked the words out, understanding what he was saying. I saw this as God's intervention. My heart swelled with compassion and a sense of purpose as I walked over to them and interrupted their discussion. I asked them to bring my little nephew to me. They both looked at me, a bit astonished because I understood them as they spoke. They were even more surprised that I was willing to take care of another son. Pélé came soon after. He had such a presence about him that I fell in love with him immediately.

I soon was known as the "Tanti" (auntie) that helped. There were older relatives, teenagers that contacted me and asked if they could stay for various reasons. There was one who just had a few years left before graduating from high school. Another, who had important school exams to complete and wanted to live closer to the institution until her tests were finished. Their parents lived too far away and my place was more convenient to get to their school using public transportation. Odette became a welcome border in my home for almost 3 years. God surely filled my cup, continuing with a few more children. After 11.5 years living overseas, I cared for seven foster children besides my two children.

I left Ivory Coast in May 1988 to resettle in the United States. My heart was very broken to get the news that two of my Abidjan family died in June of that

year, only one month after my departure. They were
Isabelle and François. Their deaths burdened my heart
greatly because I felt that if I had stayed, they might
have lived longer. Life in the Ivory Coast was so fragile.
I mourned deeply certain that my decision to leave had
impacted my children and still today my heart even
now aches.

Eight years passed and thoughts of raising children
seemed to be a vague memory and long gone. But God's
plan for my life had room for one more. I am in awe of
how He works that I have to also share this part about
my last foster child.

When I had my third loss, Lisa was two-and-a-half
years old, and she started nursery school. I felt the
depression fill my heart, and I prayed, asking why I was
having such troubles trying to have babies. My mom
had eight, and I wanted at least to have half as many. I
then realized that God opened my heart to care for the
young ones who did not have the guardianship they
needed to survive. This verse seemed to stay on my
heart for a long while;

"And whoever welcomes one such child in my name
welcomes me. Mat. 18:5".

The conversation between my brother-in-law and
my husband happened at this time. I wrote this earlier
in the story about Pélé, coming to my home.

It is my genuine belief that God so strategically

blessed me with all the cuteness of Pélè that my mind only leaped with praises and contentment. I could serve God by taking care of all the children with contentment. But Pélé's story had repeated itself, with a slight variation, which I recognized immediately as Donald's situation unfolded.

I was watching my 11-year-old son growing up with no siblings because Lisa was much older and often off on high school sports competition, leaving him to watch on the sidelines. Now being in States, our lifestyle was different. I was meditating about this, and I felt it was God's timing when a radio commercial came on talking about adopting one of the precious little 'Black Stars' in foster care. I listened carefully and wrote down the important details I needed. A few weeks later, I found myself driving up to the community center, and it was very easy to fill out the required forms for foster care. I was thinking of fostering a boy that can transition to an adaption. I requested that he would be10 years old and my son would have a playmate and my mothering urges would be blessed.

They made me aware that there were policies to abide by in my condominium park, and I needed to share my intention of adding a foster child to my family. Fostering was extra and adopting wasn't set yet. The condo park board denied my request to allow me to do this because I lived in a two bedroom and my daughter was still living at home. My heart was bigger than my house. The center respected this decision and said that when my daughter officially moved out, to please reapply. Unfortunately, the agency closed soon afterwards and the hope of adopting with that agency was lost.

I prayed, and I kept my heart busy with the children I taught in the Buffalo Public Schools. I tried not to stress on what did not happen for me. My teaching filled me and I was even entering my doctorial studies at the State University of Buffalo in the focus of Elementary Science Education. I remembered this moment like it was yesterday. I was in my second year of studies on June 28, 2001. I came home from a full day of work and post-graduate studies when God called me. I knew in my soul that I would have to obey and move on His command. My son was now 16 years old, entering his senior year in high school. It was my younger sister, Norma, who called me and urged me to return the call as soon as I could because it was extremely important. She outlined the family trauma and there was an immediate need for someone to step forward in the family court to take in my great nephew.

I walked like something else was leading me through the downtown streets of Buffalo, and I entered the courthouse. I met the judge, Honorable Judge Rosa, and she knew all about me. She was very friendly. Judge

Rosa asked if I was willing to take in my great nephew, Donald. I responded that; I was apprised of the situation, and I was ready to take on this responsibility. The next hour was a world wind of actions. I gathered all the information and my great nephew came to my home with me. I discovered he was 10 years old and my spirit echoed, "Here is the 10-year-old you needed to have." I foster cared my great nephew for almost nine years. He was my last foster child. When he graduated from high school and moved out, this was the end of me parenting children.

SPECIAL MEMORIES AND MOMENTS

My schedule was excruciatingly busy while completing my Bachelor's degree, my senior project, working a full-time job in the spring and summer, and 20 vigorous hours of a part-time work during the winter and fall. The last two semesters on top of everything else I participated in the young adult choir at church and helping my grandmother's missionary group once in a while. It was exhausting. I was engaged to be married. A lot was on my mind, especially putting out a strong effort to finish the last two semesters of college with my best grades.

I was at the peak of my performance, feeling that I was experiencing all that one could want. I was in the best physical shape, health, and felt mentally stronger than I ever was in the entire 17 years of schooling. I believed God picked me up to elevate me past the insecurities I had from my younger years and placed me in a confident spot in my educational career. One of the main reasons for such an up-lifting demeanor was I appreciated all the support my husband gave me. He was at the very top of his class at UB and he insisted that I could do the same. He motivated me to really take advantage of what I was given. This additional concentrated effort in my studies surprised me on what I was producing. Hours just flew by as I worked while I did not think about the few hours of sleep I had. My performance was rated highly by my professors, which was a major change from previous years of schooling.

But, sadly that higher stress level could have been a factor as to why I lost the babies. The same compounded situation in my life at the time became the additional pressures for me living in Abidjan was a great challenge as well. There were different degrees of stress of higher work concentration and maintaining a single-parent household in Abidjan. My husband mostly worked in other countries and not in our home city, were factors not measured completely. My two doctors made no assumptions or any thoughts of lacking of any kind were ever spoken. Plus, I did not think to say anything; I was silently managing my life and stress. Thinking back to those many moments, I reflected on how I saw myself spiritually. I ask if I was standing on all what I learned and believed. I was doing the best I could humanly muster up, and I saw many signs of God picking me up and carrying through. I truly believed that I was caring for God's special little ones for the moment they were in my supervision, on this earth.

Just like Pélé's arrival to my home, I saw space for one more and I prayed, asking God if He wanted to fill it. I felt that I was expecting again. Some would say that I sounded a little off, but I laughed to myself and said in my prayers assuredly You will fill my cup once more. So, I repeated the conversation with my brother-in-law several years later about who else was in the village that was left from the family. I thought, if there was another, God would have him tell me about this child. My in-law came to me after he checked to see and spoke about a twin girl named Isabelle whose sister was already staying with his niece in Abidjan for over a year now. He warned me that the sister was difficult to work with and being a twin, Isabelle might be a hand full as well. I prayed and asked for wisdom because my heart naively and immediately thought of a sweet reunion of twin sisters. I felt the sun's warmth inside me as I was meditating on her name. Soon after, I told him to talk to her to see if she wanted to come. A few weeks later, I was told she was coming. Isabelle did a self-tour through-out my home with giant eyes and a huge dimpled grin on her face. Isabelle came to me speaking only Dida, but my spirit knew what she was saying. She embraced me with a love filled hug, thanking Jesus for granting her a way to come live with her aunt. My in-law said that Pélé and Odette could translate for me. She returned to the living room where I was sitting, and Pélé spoke for her. She asked what she could do first. I noticed she wore no shoes but my in-law advised me to do nothing about that right away. I brought all the chil-dren together and introduced each one. I thought this was interesting, that my birth daughter, Lisa, was the only one in the group that did not understand or speak Dida well. I thought Lisa was going to get it with that much exposure. The first request I made; Isabelle was the oldest, beside Odette. She would be in charge. Everyone was to continue to maintain the family rules guiding her until she knows. Isabelle was a natural leader, and she assumed responsibility of her cousins with thoughtfulness. The children seemed to welcome her immediately. They blended well right away. By eight pm that first night, all the children were fed, had their baths, and in bed reading their books. Isabelle wanted to be a part of my home and I was going to nurture a strong family connection with her without spoiling her.

I sat with her and Odette that evening, talking to her about what her life was like in the village. Her story was very sad. She became very emotional with us as she spoke. Odette and I comforted her and assured her that we cared and would help her. She and her twin were the youngest in her family. She had other cousins that she lived with because her parents had passed away. Her main desire at that time was to get a pair of flip-flops to wear when she went out. She would walk around bare-footed in the house. I bought her a few necessary clothes and the slippers. She was clean, and I never had to get on her about washing her clothes or taking baths. She was completely opposite of her twin sister.

I was amazed by her when she came to me after getting all her chores done; while the children were in school, she shared with me the schedule of a literacy and vocational program she wanted to attend. She thought she could go back to school while her cousins were in school. I had Odette go with her and they found out how she could sign-up for the classes. She was registered and started classes; she started her remedial math and reading and one vocational course the next week. Isabelle did the sewing classes first and became a good sewer after a year. The next classes were training her to become a midwife. She wanted to stay with this and took a series of classes along with her academic courses. She completed up to her sixth-grade exams and passed them all by the time I was preparing to return to the States in 1988. I returned to the States and Isabelle found herself with no family to take her in. She had to go back to the village with no main source of income. Living in extreme poverty in the village, Isabelle died of an illness a month later. Isabelle, I miss you so much.

FRANÇOIS

I just became a new resident in the country of Ivory Coast in 1976 and getting used to the major changes in the life-style. The spring of 1977 I got into the habit of watching the president of the country chat to his constituents at the noon hour on TV on Saturdays. The President of Ivory Coast, His Excellency Félix Houphouët-Boigny was lecturing about what is a very important duty for all the educated and well-educated residents of the country should do to assist the poor and needy. I became interested in his "fireside chat" and pulled up a chair to listen more intensely. He spoke about his country not having the wealth like the big Western ones and could not afford welfare programs, but we as a nation could develop a welfare network amongst ourselves to take care of our relatives. I had supported this attitude even in the states before I came there. I was happy that the president encouraged this amongst the Ivoirians, so that I would not have to think of a convincing argument to present to my husband about looking within his family to get our new house worker because the first one did not do well.

My husband had a giant smile on his face as I spoke about what I heard on the news that afternoon and before I could pose the question he said, "Yes," with a big embrace. He said he was proud of how well I was adjusting in his country. So, I spoke to my sister-in-law, this was my husband's older sister, about finding the right one. Shortly afterwards, she called me to come to her house and meet François, who was 15 years old. He lived far away in an impoverished suburb of the main city, Abidjan, but worked around his family's home. The family arranged for him to live with his cousin, who was closer, so he could work. François was introduced to me as a distant relative to my husband, who had done little in his studies but was a hard worker. I was told to treat him as one of my own and go over all the basic life habits like how to wash up and brush your teeth. Also, remind him to change the bucket of water regularly so that he was not using dirty water. He was eager to work and asked, in his broken French, many questions. That already told me that he was bright and just did not have the chance of proper schooling.

He got along with the rest of the children immediately because he would gather them in their play room to tell them why it was important to pick up their toys. He had their complete attention and as I watched, I thought; he was a big brother in his family's home. My children adapted to him instantly because they would make sure they fixed a lunch sandwich for him when they made theirs.

The funniest time was when Lisa was around 2 years old and she was transiting out of her diapers. She would take her diaper off, take the wet diaper and immediately run to François's bucket to drop it in. He would scold her that the water was not for her diaper but for daddy's dress shirts. She got his attention doing pranks like that and the games continued with a series of escapes on how she could sneak behind his back with something to throw in his pail. She was caught sitting in his bucket since he was catching her too quickly, stopping her from throwing her diapers in the bucket. François's patience began to wear thin when he started to yell at her, but stopped short. I took Lisa into the other room and set the boundaries on what she could do.

Lisa cried and sat in the hallway, watching him. François finished his work and still found Lisa sitting there. He went and found her baby bathtub and filled it with water. He put her toys inside and got Lisa to sit in the tub while he ironed the dried clothes. This became the ritual between Lisa and him for several months. As she played and sang in her tub, he would try to learn all her rhymes and songs. He was definitely going to be a great father one day; I thought to myself.

When François turned 20 years old, he came to me with a very serious attitude and wanted to talk privately with me. We sat silently for a moment and he was a little nervous and I refused to try and guess what he wanted. He had been with my family for more than five years now, and I feared he was going to say that he was moving on to a different job. He was awkward as he spoke and started to hesitate a little, then slowly he began to express his message. He said he felt that he was a man now ready to take a wife and wanted to get married. He asked me how he should do with his to be wife. My heart burst with joy thinking my daughter was around six years old and I had a young adult son talking about marriage. I gave him the overview of the numerous examples I saw in him of how he would make a great husband and father, but I told him my point of view came from a foreigner's lifestyle and perspective. So, I told him it would be better for him to talk to my husband or brother-in-law. He did and several months later; he was married. Within the next five years he had two sons and one baby coming.

Then, a few months after his third son was born, he was hired to a very good job offer from the American embassy. I was now resettled in the USA. Then, inexplicably, Francoise died shortly afterwards. God, my beloved Francoise, is in your arms.

MY GRIEF JOURNEY

I wrote about the entire process and steps God took to give me the family that I had hoped and prayed for because I was presenting the complete picture which helped me deal with all my losses. I felt God's blessings through-out this journey as well as the emotional pain. I understood the well being that breathed into my spirit and body that I looked forward to why and how my life was going to bloom and flourish. I also felt the depression invade my presence as I watched a continuous line of a large family passing me. Yes, I did grieve over not having all of my own babies.

The very youthful dreams and pleasures danced with an abundance of energy in my mind was a contrast reality to the maturing spirit nurturing my wisdom to comprehend God's plan for me all was intertwining at the most rapid speed. I could feel this divine touch on me. My life's experience was preparing me to write my life's story. When my heavenly Father saw my strength, He wanted to use it to build my testimony and prepare me for my spiritual walk.

This was a process, but this is how I coped with the

deaths of all my babies. I was always seeking the bigger picture that I truly believed that God was painting for me and preparing for me. I saw in the faces and spirits of my adoptive family the spark of life that was meant to shine. I loved them for it. I loved the life they gave me. I felt God's love through them. I am so thankful to have known my adoptive children and I continue to pray for the ones who are still living; Odette, Lydie, Pélé, Donald, Ahou, and Chantelle. The hurt, the pain, the joy and the love, all this kept me filled and completely seeking God's plan for me.

Something amazing happened recently a few weeks ago while I was writing this story. Even after all my children are grown and living their own lives, I can still sit and remember the pains of my past. I was going through one of those tender moments and God stood toe to toe with me, helping me feel the peace of His comfort. I was in another room and could hear the TV show "Ask the Pastor"; on TCT was playing. I overheard the question where someone was asking about when your babies die. I ran into the room to listen and hear more about what was being said. It felt like God was broadcasting through this program and I was present because the question was exactly all about me, I thought. It said that someone lost FIVE pregnancies like me and the mother wanted to know if she would see her babies in heaven. I cried fresh tears at that moment. The answer was:

YES!!!! I WILL SEE ALL MY FIVE BABIES IN HEAVEN. PRAISE THE LORD!!!

6

SEVEN OF SUDDENLY

AKEA HOLLINGSWORTH

No one ever prepares for child loss. We prepare for the birth with birthing plans, nurseries, showers, their tiny needs, the labor and if you are on top of your game, their college fund. But never a death, never!!! Because losing a child is unnatural, it's not the natural order of things. Even in scripture, a father to the fatherless, a defender of widows, is God in His holy dwelling {Psalms 68:5}. As I know of there isn't a scripture for a motherless child. We know Mary had to witness her son Jesus' death, which was horrifying. What do I do without my child? There is not even a title for a parent without their child. A child without a parent is an orphan, a husband without a wife is a widower, a wife without her husband is a widow.

Maya was my only child, so that loss makes it different as well. No parent, even if you have more than one, decides, "well if I had to lose a child, this should be the one". But the blessing is having another at least. Then the question comes up, "how many children do you have or do you have children"? Hmm, what do I say? I would be stumped and tripping over what to say, especially when I didn't want to admit that Maya was in fact not here, not on earth, she was dead, deceased, passed away, gone, in Heaven, with God; all those she was. My answer was always one and yes, I have a child. There were no if, ands or buts about it. But what am I? Am I still a mother? Yes, and always will be. And my answer now is I have one, and she is my angel.

Let's start with Maya's birth; Due date July 5, 1999, but she was born on Sunday July 18th. She was exactly 2 weeks past her due date that day and she was a true OVERDUE baby. She had every physical sign of an overdue baby. I swear she looked like she was two months, ok maybe I'm exaggerating but definitely one month, holding her head already, eight pounds, 21 inches, dry skin, wrinkled belly and HUNGRY!! Did I mention the girl was hungry, coming out sucking the side of her hand? She came, healthy, big and again HUNGRY! She was perfect, black hair, she looked like a doll baby who would once in a while "smile" at angels. But she came into this world on her terms. She was comfy, in her correct position to come out, head down, legs just moving back and forth. My girl was chilling, would not move much besides that, and content.

The doctors would use this apparatus that buzzed and it would stimulate her, but she would go right back in chill mode. I was induced; my induction started on a Friday with Cervidil, which is a suppository used to stimulate or start labor. Each dose is 12 hours; I had TWO!! Then I got the big dawg (meant to spell that way), Pitocin. If you have never been induced with the "Pit" then thank heavens because those contractions come back to back. By the time it's coming down, another is right behind it. Well, even though that finally worked, it didn't work enough. I went to seven centimeters only, after losing blood and oxygen level dropping, it was decided that I get a Cesarean. For sure, she was stubborn and going to be one to be reckoned with, proven just by her entry into the world. I instantly named her Maya (after Maya Angelou) when I found out I was having a girl only a short month or so before having her. I wanted a girl really, really bad! I thought if I was having a girl, the name was going to be Jasmine. As soon as I knew, it changed instantly to Maya when I got home from the appointment. Then, not knowing if I would have another child or even another girl, so I gave her the middle name, Marguerita. It was a combination of my mother's name and grandmother's name, Elreda and Marguerite, not the drink. Geez, I just was just a year shy of being legal guys.

We were in the hospital for a week, and a day, about five days after I had her, I ended up with a respiratory infection. We seemed like residents by that time, and she was affectionately known as M&M by the nurses. I was so happy to be a mom that I kept her in my room most of the time until I got sick. I was only three weeks from my twenty-second birthday. She was my early birthday present and my new reality, including postpartum depression. I thought I was crazy when the nurse just mentioned formula, and I cried, or when I was getting discharged, I cried.

But as long and painful as the labor was, my real and hardest job was coming. I was now a single, POOR, partially educated mom. I had dropped out of college where I was getting my Bachelor of science in Child and Youth Services at a private college; I was scared, trying to work. I dropped out too early and if I had stayed in school, there would have been all kinds of help for me. But Akea is strong willed, determined, hard-headed, "I can do it myself" woman... I thought I can learn the newest hot thing and provide for my child. It was easier to think and say than to do.

Maya was such a good baby after and in between the

colic phase, geez. She had a cry that sounded like a laugh, but her real laugh was just the sweetest thing. She was my precious chipmunk and my first love.

Well, single mom and working mom were in full effect, learning the ropes of daycare, social services and balancing work and school. I went to Bryant and Stratton for a short time after she was newly born, but it became too difficult to do, so again, I chose work. I started as a temp at the NYS Health Department; it was by far the best job, because of Maya's colic, the daycare would call frequently to come get her or she would get sick because of being in daycare and this job allowed me to bring Maya to work with me. When I worked, my co-workers would take turns with her. It was a temporary job, and I had to look for a permanent job. Before I left, I was shown how appreciated I was with a party, gifts, and a shopping spree by the lawyer who I worked under. At the time customer service was becoming big, you could make a salary of an entry level college degreed person. I started at a dial up company as a billing /customer service representative then moved on to the cable company. Maya grew up, from the ages of two to nine, with my coworkers, whom many became like family.

She was so sweet and caring. As a toddler, she would swear every man she saw was "daddy", she was a hoot. I would say by the age of three or four, she was a jokester, loved to play practical jokes on me and could act very well. She knew I was sensitive if she were hurt, so she thought it was funny to "cry" and make up something and then get me all upset and then burst out laughing. She was a total trip. She was a songbird, she sang very well. I don't know where she got it from because as much as I love to sing, I cannot sing. She loved Beyonce, Taylor Swift and Hannah Montana (Little Miley Cyrus) and those around that time popular with her age group. I just knew she was going to be a singer and actress, especially Broadway and Stage. We went to see several plays, her favorite Hairspray (she watched the DVD movie a million times) and just about two weeks before she got sick, we went to see Color Purple.

She was well loved in school, never had a behavior issue, and she excelled when she could after a lot of tough love. Whew, that girl tried my patience with math… 1 plus 3, her answer: 7???? "Girl"…. that girl!! I would take those days back in a heartbeat.

THE SUDDENLY... EARTHQUAKE AND TSUNAMI IN ONE

On June 12, 2009, we woke up to what I thought would be a regular Friday. It was close to the end of the school year and Maya was looking forward to her last trip of that school year to see the Lockport Locks, part of the Erie Canal, which is in Lockport, NY. She was so excited that I was excited for her. She woke up with a typical sore throat, "Oh, Maya, it's probably allergies but if I give you Benadryl, you will get sleepy, so let's see how things go". Maya was so disappointed she did not go on her trip because she ended up having to be with our aunt that day. As the day progressed, she eventually got a fever and "I really don't feel good."

I get her after work; I go to buy the medicine, that is normally bought for cold and flu and orange juice. Again, we had spent the first two years or so dealing with viruses, ear infections, ear tube surgeries, adenoid removal and tonsillectomy surgery too, but by the time she was school age, her immune system was very strong.

By that evening I am thinking maybe it could be "Swine Flu" but we have gone nowhere. We had been using our hand sanitizer. I made sure Maya had her own supply. She had been using it and washing her hands and I was CLEAN. She even started making her own (the hand sanitizer) by mixing Bath and Body Works lotions with the sanitizer so her hands would be moisturized. I told you she was so smart. We had already had a pcp appointment set the next day, Saturday. But when my baby, who I was very over protective over, who was nine, almost ten and almost as tall as me, started having serious palpitations and tachycardia while laying down resting. I saw her pulse in her neck and was getting about 150 beats per minute. After calling 911, the EMS was getting about 165 bpm. When we got to the hospital, she seemed to be ok and playing with one of my childhood friend's daughter in the waiting room of the ER, which was swamped. She was there for the same reason and both tested positive for Strain A influenza. Because they tested positive, the results were supposed to be sent to the Erie County Health Department, as told by the provider. Remember this tidbit of information!!!

The following day, it seems like Maya was feeling better. We had oatmeal for breakfast. She went on the computer and then felt run down again. She laid in my bed to rest, again my spoiled baby as she was not supposed to be. Now this is Saturday, the doctor's appointment was canceled because we already confirmed for influenza and told to quarantine for seven days. On this day, as reality was setting in, I started sanitizing the shared hallway with our neighbors and also our home.

Sunday, day three progressed, "mom, I can't breathe, my chest hurts". A call to her PCP and she has her concerns. By this time the ER's are packed still and the PCP says you need to go back because she may have pneumonia and did I mention that by this time I'm sick as well. I feel like pure awful. Her pediatrician knew some of my history with asthma and suggested that this Children's Hospital see my grown butt. Thinking they would give me Tamiflu and her a chest x-ray. She got her chest x-ray hours later, by this time she was declining and it was thought she was just "tired" and may have bronchitis? Her x-ray was clear, however she just went to sleep. We arrived and triaged about ten pm and were not seen until about 2 or 3 in the morning. My baby was literally dying, and I had no idea. And as for me, I was told I had an upper respiratory infection, so basically a cold. My question to the provider was how can I have a cold from the flu? Which we knew for sure she had. This example is one of many I've had and millions of others have that shows how our medical providers do not listen to us as persons of color and as a woman of color. It's thought that we can take pain more, and that needs to be changed. I am blessed to have extensive medical knowledge just because of real-life experiences and then I also was working at a health insurance company. I wasn't uneducated. I had private health insurance, but that didn't matter. I was just what they thought: a poor, uneducated black single mom who was overreacting. The ER was swamped and most cases were flu related because in 2009 the H1N1 epidemic was affecting children. Even though on that particular date she was not confirmed, H1N1 or "Swine

Flu" because remember we had to wait for confirmation from the health department, again more coming on that one.

We arrive home. She is just so lethargic. I had to keep waking her to drink and eating was out of the question. I am trying to medicate myself with her, and at this point, we are both down. At one point, I was coughing, and she patted me on my back in her weak state. Again, she was the sweetest angel.

Another three hours or so, declining, breathing is fast. By Tuesday June 16th, I told Maya we have to go. It was very early in the morning, maybe around five or six. When she woke a little, she could see straight through me it seemed and her tongue was all white. My daughter was dying, and I had no idea.

When we arrived at Children's hospital, EMS grabbed her right away and carried her. She was assessed right away. We discussed what the last few days had been from that past Friday to this current Tuesday morning. I told the attending physician that she was positive strain A, and we were waiting for confirmation on the H1N1. He then said to me "all of those strain A's have been coming back positive for Swine Flu, as the normal Strain A should be dead by now, its now June 16th and they stopped testing those." So can you imagine my shock? "You have the sickest child in WNY, right now," came out of his mouth a few

minutes later. Here I am by myself and in total disbelief.
It seemed I was having an out-of-body experience. This
is all within fifteen to twenty minutes of arriving at the
hospital.

Now I had to understand not only how seriously
and critically sick she was but discuss options on how
to save her, "Bipap, Oxygen sats (oxygen saturations),
Ventilator and we don't have long" was all a part of that
conversation regarding the decision. It was decided that
she was too sick for Bipap as her oxygen was very, very
low, in the low seventies and low eighties, and she was
almost non-responsive. She was then immediately put
on a ventilator and just before she was ventilated, I was
able to go talk with her and tell her everything was
going to be ok and that I loved her even though inside I
wasn't too sure. I was scared as shit then! She was
immediately sedated after I was walked out of the
room.

A few hours had then passed by, some family had
come and we were now in the Pediatric ICU and I had
the endless questions asked; Did you travel to Mexico
or outside the country? Have you traveled anywhere,
were you around anyone who was sick? The questions
asked were pretty much all the questions that many are
used to now with this Covid pandemic. No, NO, NO
NO, were my answers, but I wanted to scream; inside I
was screaming. I wanted to be by my Maya's side. We

were always together, just save my baby, I screamed and thought. If answering these stupid questions was going to save her, I was willing to do it, but damn, they were getting on my nerves.

In that short time after, despite Maya being ventilated, and the ventilator was at the highest setting and she was totally depending on the ventilator and not doing any breathing on her own. One of the best PICU trauma doctors was on our team, as well as his wife. Another quick decision had to be made. Maya needed ECMO (Extracorporeal Membrane Oxygenation), she was only still at an eighty percent oxygenation rate. Which would put her at risk of going brain dead within a few hours. At that time, she was only one of the first ten people they had used the ECMO on as advanced life support. ECMO is the same machine that is used when someone has a heart or lung transplant and it oxygenates the blood and acts as the heart and lungs do. It is a very complicated machine and actually took a special team to handle it. The easiest way to describe this life saving machine in many cases is that it's like a dialysis machine.

As they were explaining to me how serious and critical Maya was and signing, it seemed, Maya's life away on paper, they realized they could not take Maya only a few feet down the hall to put her on this complicated machine; she was too unstable. As they were prepping to do this surgery-like procedure, I didn't get the chance to go see her, so I had to just wait and pray. As they were getting her on the machine, she went into cardiac arrest three times. Each time the doctor, who was the wife of the other pediatrician, would come back to the parent room with tear-filled eyes as a mother herself and hoping but realistically in her voice showing hope was all lost, as she was telling me that Maya arrested the third time. They got Maya on the ECMO, which by the way took up two ICU rooms, numbers three and four, to be exact. Remember those numbers. They then later told me how they were doing manual chest compressions the whole while. The cardiologist said he was not a person of faith but used mine to "guide" him and how Maya's arteries felt and what he learned because usually this ECMO has to use imaging to make sure the right arteries are used. Maya was so complicated they placed the tubing in her arteries, in her neck and her groin.

As Maya was going into arrest, I asked for a clergy so we can pray while they worked on my daughter "I don't care if it's a Rabbi, Priest or Preacher" I said. I knew we all believe in one God and that was all I cared about and as the scriptures says "For when two or three are gathered in my name" (Matt 18:20 KJV), heck I didn't care if Budda himself was all they had, a connection was a connection to God.

Well, they sent a chaplain, who introduced himself to me and my family as Reverend Campbell. We prayed and after Maya was placed on the advanced life support, he graciously offered his contact info and wrote on a business card as well. As he's handing it to me, all I can think is "black people know we write our numbers on anything". Well, as I am looking at the name it says Dr. Luther Campbell, so I finally had a "duh" moment and asked "are you, a doctor?". He replied, "Yes, I am". Well, because of the seriousness of Maya, none of us were allowed back in her room despite me begging, but he was able to go back there and pray over the doctors, as they still worked on her. So despite the sadness, seriousness and critical stage my angel was in, God was present despite of. Here is a quick rundown of our team; we had the most experienced trauma pediatrician who had published the latest medical book for Pediatric Intensive Care that was being used by medical schools all over the country, his wife who was well credentialed and experienced and then our "chaplain" who was a minister and an endocrinologist.

As today's pandemic, even though it was not nearly as many people who succumbed or infected, it was always in the news and "hot" until at least half the summer. Per the CDC, it was estimated that between 151,700 and 575, 000 people died worldwide of H1N1 and there were 12,469 deaths in the US, globally about eighty percent were of people under the age of sixty-five. *CDC.Gov* Maya was believed to be the 71st child to have passed away from the virus.

We were told that Maya would be critical for at least 3 weeks and would probably be under extensive rehabilitation. As the days progressed, it was realized that she was septic and her circulatory and respiratory system was affected, namely her heart and lungs. The realization that if this angel survived, she would then also need both a heart and lung transplant. Dealing with all this and still having to deal with real life was difficult. Since it seemed Maya would be a resident of the hospital, I then had to decide if I can go back to work as they wanted me back and how would I spent every night there in the parent room, quarantined with my family and loved ones as I was infected with the flu as well. We would literally have air mattresses up all night, eat and then clean up so other parents can use the parent room along with us (after my quarantine was up) and luckily, no one was sick from me.

More days passed by, the stress was becoming a lot for the doctors, nurses and hospital staff. Maya and by that time another child were both critically ill, both on ECMO and they required a lot of donated blood. A local blood/organ bank set up an area for blood donation. I thank God for the people who donated, as well as the staff who mobilized the drive for several days. I also got to sit with friends in the ER as their kids were sick with the flu or at least displaying symptoms. The ER still looked like a war zone, people sitting everywhere and no room in the waiting room. The news is spreading; the news is camped outside. This was the first time dealing with the media and the hospital's press advisor letting me know how to handle them or if I want them to handle the media. Then finally, I spoke with the news when it seemed misinformation was given as it pertained to how Maya contracted the flu. Maya contracted her flu from school. I wanted the public to know that the virus was in our schools.

I spoke to more doctors than I ever imagined in my life, even with having a very sick mother and being her caregiver. I was her caregiver until her death, from my mid-teens to 19 years old. I spoke with infectious disease doctors who were baffled and even baffled at the fact I had a "cold" when I even knew that wasn't possible. So I was tested and of course I tested positive, but by that time my symptoms were almost diminished besides my coughing and some swelling. In fact, I didn't have a confirmation of a positive test result until the day before Maya died.

Eleven days Maya fought, she fought the machine; she had blood clotted lungs which weren't relieved like we were hoping for from the last treatment tried. Her body would swell, then she had necrosis on several parts of her body. She bled from every mucous membrane of her body, and on the eleventh day, she finally got tired. The most advanced life support could not keep her alive. It was fighting with her, stopping and her blood clotting, causing it to stop. Around seven in the morning on June 27, 2009, the PA came in and told me Maya was ready to go to heaven with the information I gave you above. The PA also lost a child which influenced her to go into medicine, so she knew what I was going through. I was so in shock; I didn't know what to do. I went in her room to tell her Good Morning, like I always did, and made sure I always smelled like our favorite Bath and Body Works, but this time I told her I would be right back. I tried to pretend it was another regular morning. I went and showered and put on my scents and a new outfit I had bought the day before, as that was my only day outside the hospital for a couple of hours.

I called everyone to tell them today was the day Maya was going to heaven and I would eventually have to turn the machine off. I thought it would be an all day process. "Maya's is about to go into cardiac arrest" was told to me by the PA as we had been singing and talking to her, we sang "Never Would Have Made it" by Marvin Sapp. But as the PA said cardiac arrest, all I could imagine was the first day we were there on June sixteenth and how painful that may have been. My mom had a massive heart attack and survived it, and I could remember how badly she said it hurt. I didn't want my baby to have that again. The machine was turned off, the nurses turned the monitor from my sight, and it was called. She was gone. All I wanted to do was hold her, which I did after they cleaned her and removed most of the tubing. Dead weight is heavy, and she was so long but alive she would jump across my lap like she was a baby and that was almost a daily thing, especially after work. Well, this was it, no more "Mommy, can I go to Ajanae's house, can she come over?" Actually, they would not ask; those two would have their own plans or her friend Kerry would ring our bell because she and Maya would have planned the visit. No more of that, which got on my nerves, but I was a sucker every time for it. At that moment Maya was nine years, eleven months and twenty-one days old, FOREVER.

MY only child was now gone, and now I have to plan her funeral. Again, not the natural order of how life is supposed to happen. Her favorite color was purple because she copied off mom (me, that's my story and I'm sticking to it because before her favorite color was pink), but she loved purple. She LOVED Beyonce. Her favorite Beyonce songs were HALO and Diva. Halo fit perfectly as her latest likeness. She and God knew she was about to be my guardian angel. Maya's purple HALO shines on forever. July 2, 2009, was the final goodbye and her sermon was titled "SUDDENLY" "HAPPY BIRTHDAY". HALO was also played as we walked out behind her casket at the church. Then that following January, her class did a memorial for her and wore purple and sang HALO. IF BEY had heard of her story or saw the video, I'm sure it would have had her crying and it would have touched her heart. As I'm typing this, it's with wet eyes. My allergies came on suddenly.

Suddenly, a mysterious virus attacked my daughter along with MRSA. She was a rarity with her severity of both, one of 3 in the world most likely. She was a case study in medical journals. She changed the world in her own way and led research on the flu shot, MRSA and critical care. She always wanted to be a Broadway Star. We would watch the Tony's. She got her stardom just on the heavenly side and differently on earth's side. She is my only child, but she is my SEVEN of Suddenly. Born June 18, 1999 at 11:37pm, she was in room 3 and 4 in the hospital (I told you to pay attention). She died June 27, 2009. And since her 10th birthday was near after her death, we let up ten balloons and 3 got stuck in the tree and only SEVEN went up.

And me, SEVEN months later I was diagnosed with cancer, a rarer form of sarcoma in my upper right thigh. I was so in shock after her death and handled in "too good", well that was only because God knew I was about to face another battle because according to my oncologist was definitely there then but my strength was needed. After being diagnosed February 2010 and it removed, by her year anniversary, I felt like I had just experienced her death again. But I am now eleven years cancer free.

There is a God, and life may not be peaches and cream, even after experiencing tragedies. You will have the strength and tenacity to go through ANYTHING. Child loss is so unfair and I still question God, but when I do, I refer to this scripture; "Trust in the Lord with all your heart and lean not unto your own understanding, in all your ways submit to him and he will make your paths straight"-Proverbs 3:5-6 NIV.

Also, In closing my chapter in this marvelous work, I know there are so many who now understand exactly what I went through as about 600,000 Americans alone have now experienced Coronavirus (Covid-19) and millions more with the virus which many are still suffering even though they survived it. Worldwide, millions have experienced what I have because of this virus. I pray my story encourages you in some way and it doesn't have to be in loss. If you have never lost a child but to know with God, all things are possible. With life's challenges that seem to be ongoing for me, namely my health, I tell God, "Don't move my Mountains, just give me the strength to climb".... Keep Climbing!

EPILOGUE

I hope you are applauding these women for their bravery as they live through these stories once again to share them with you. These women have the loss of a child in common, but each of our journeys is different.

Our destinies differ, and how we grieve also differs, but the one thing that remains the same for all of us is the love that we have for our child. The pain will never disappear, but how we live our lives will change. We will celebrate our children every chance that we get. We will replace some of our tears with smiles generated from the precious memories that we have. This book is a tribute to our Angels. We are parents pushing past our grief!!

www.ingramcontent.com/pod-product-compliance
Lightning Source LLC
Chambersburg PA
CBHW071952100426

42736CB00043B/3075